MOSES AND EGYPT EXODUS COLORING BOOK

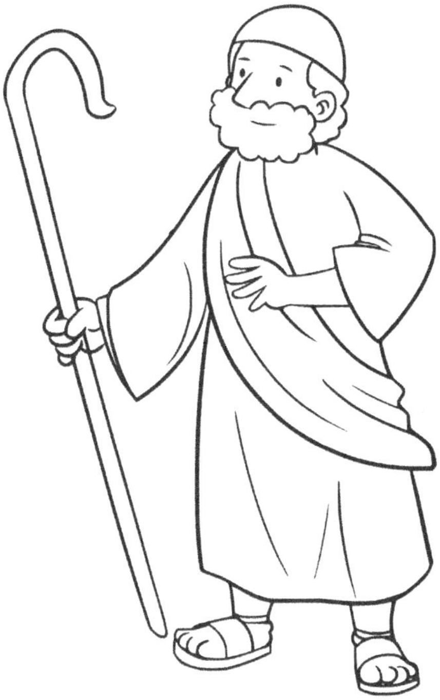

Belongs to:

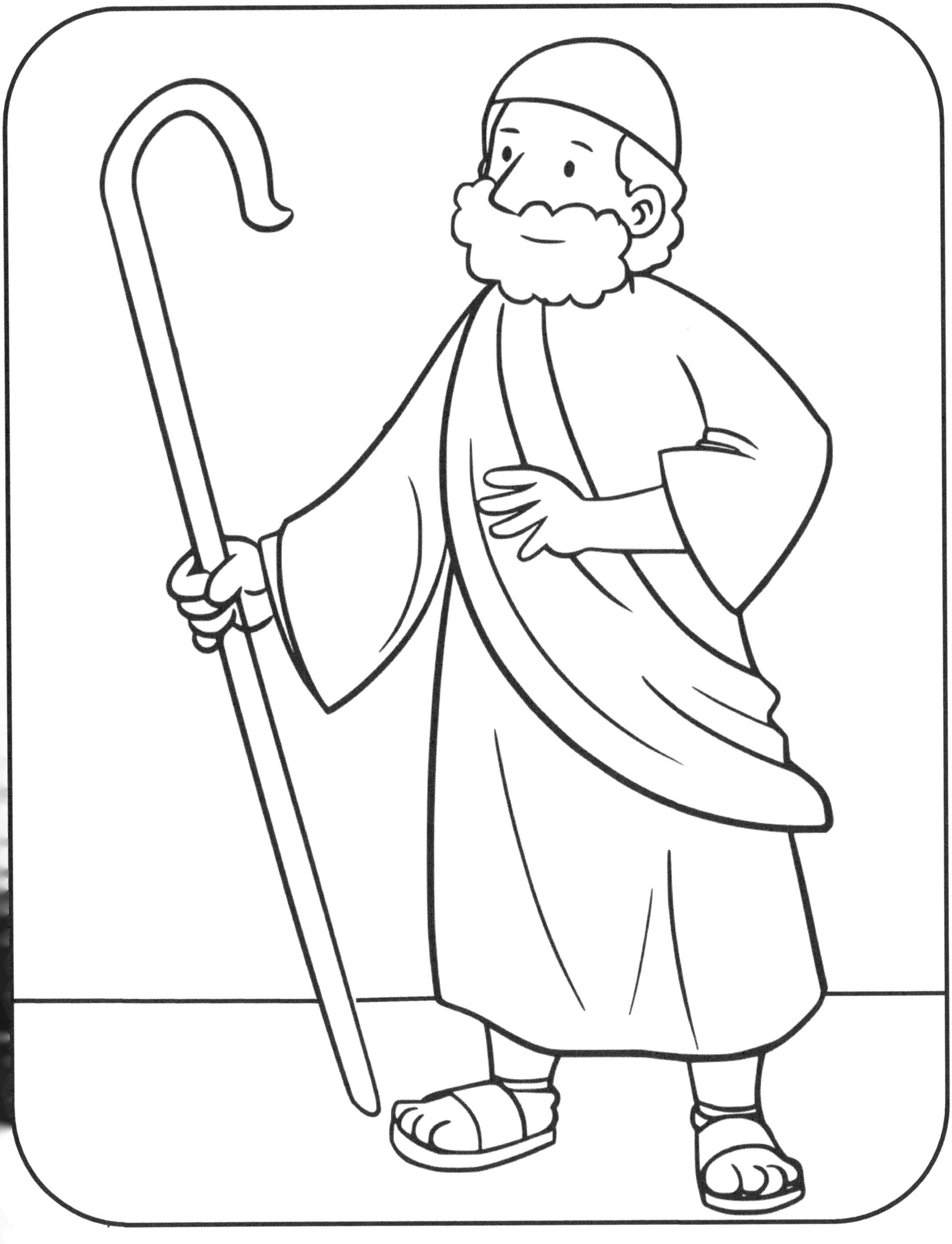

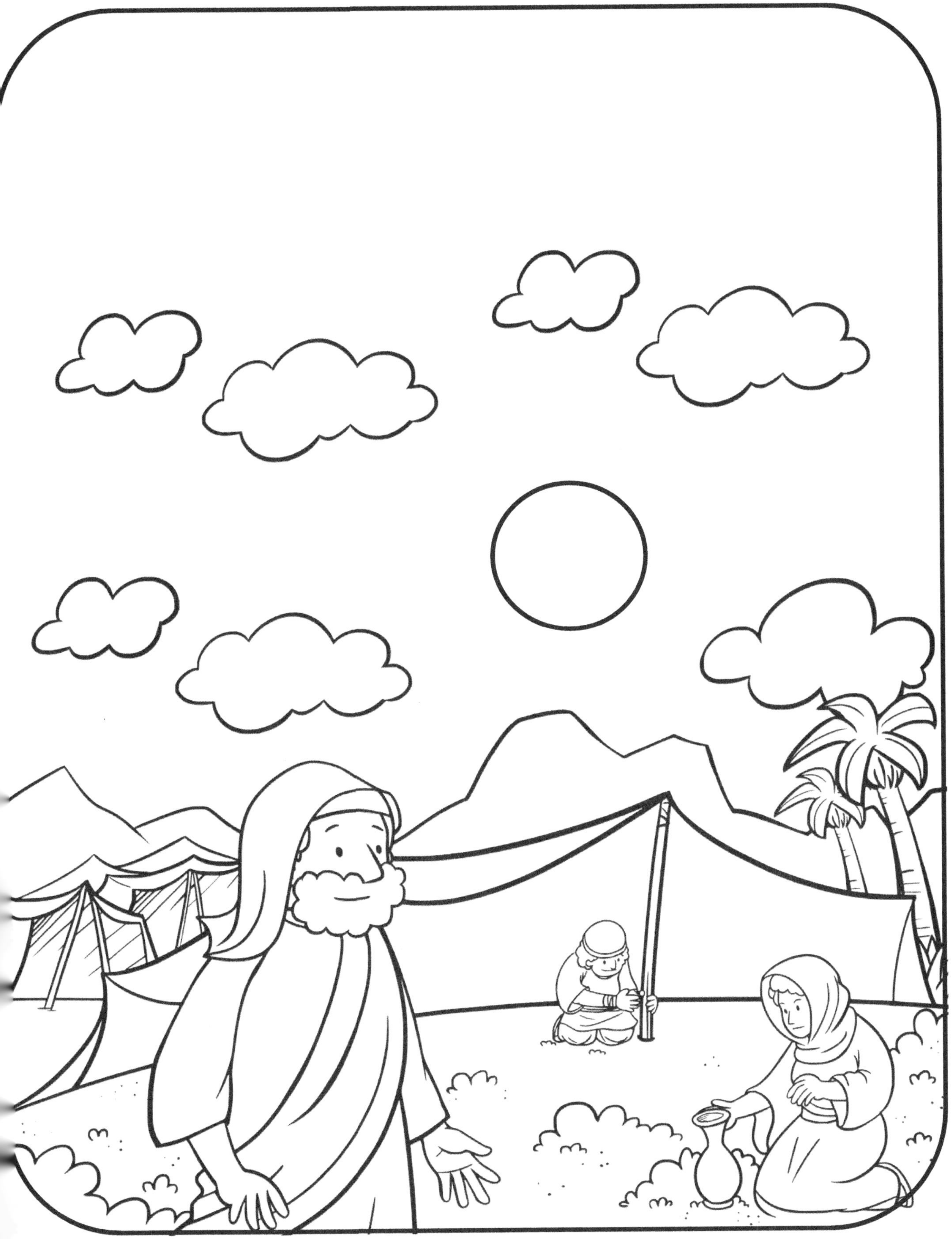

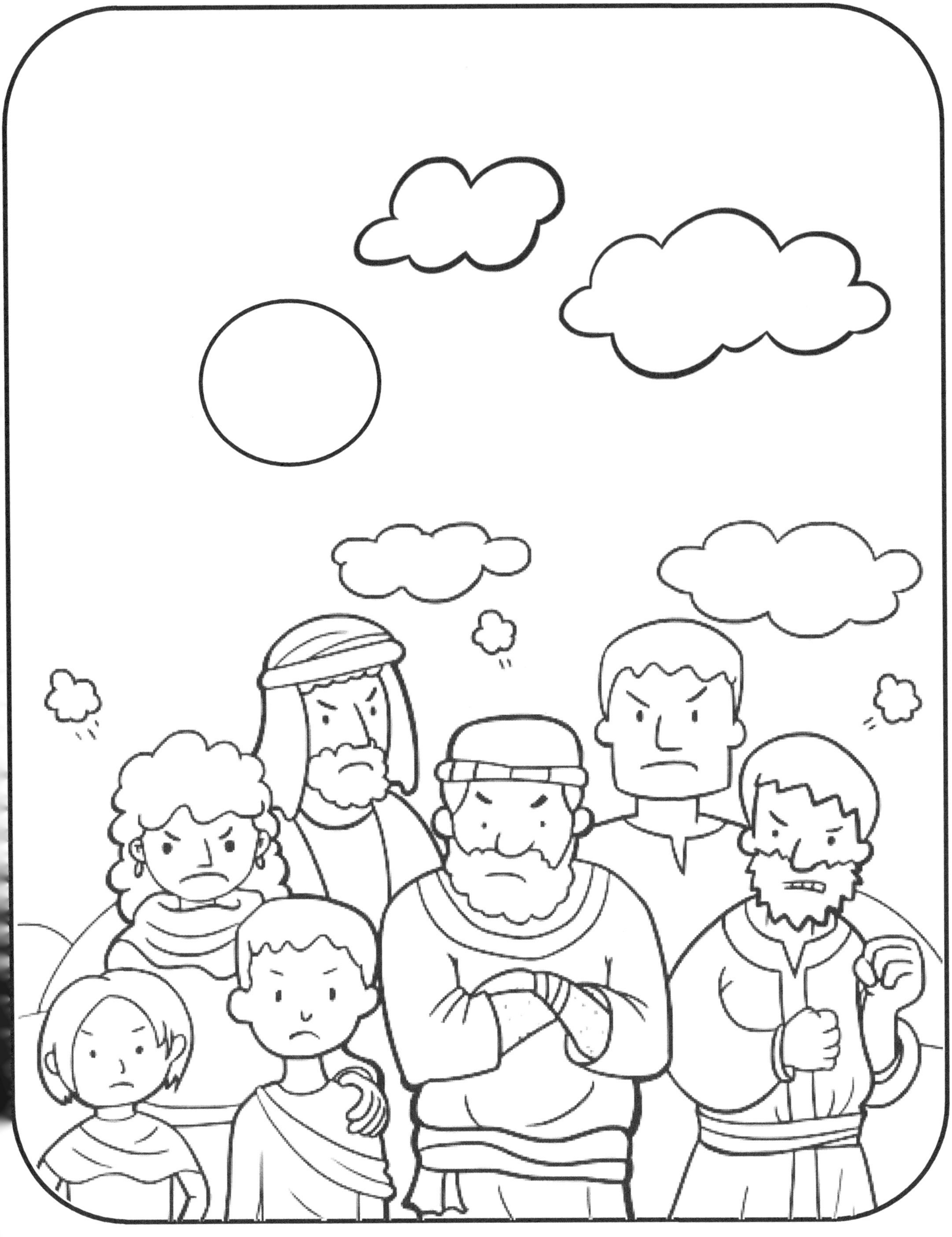

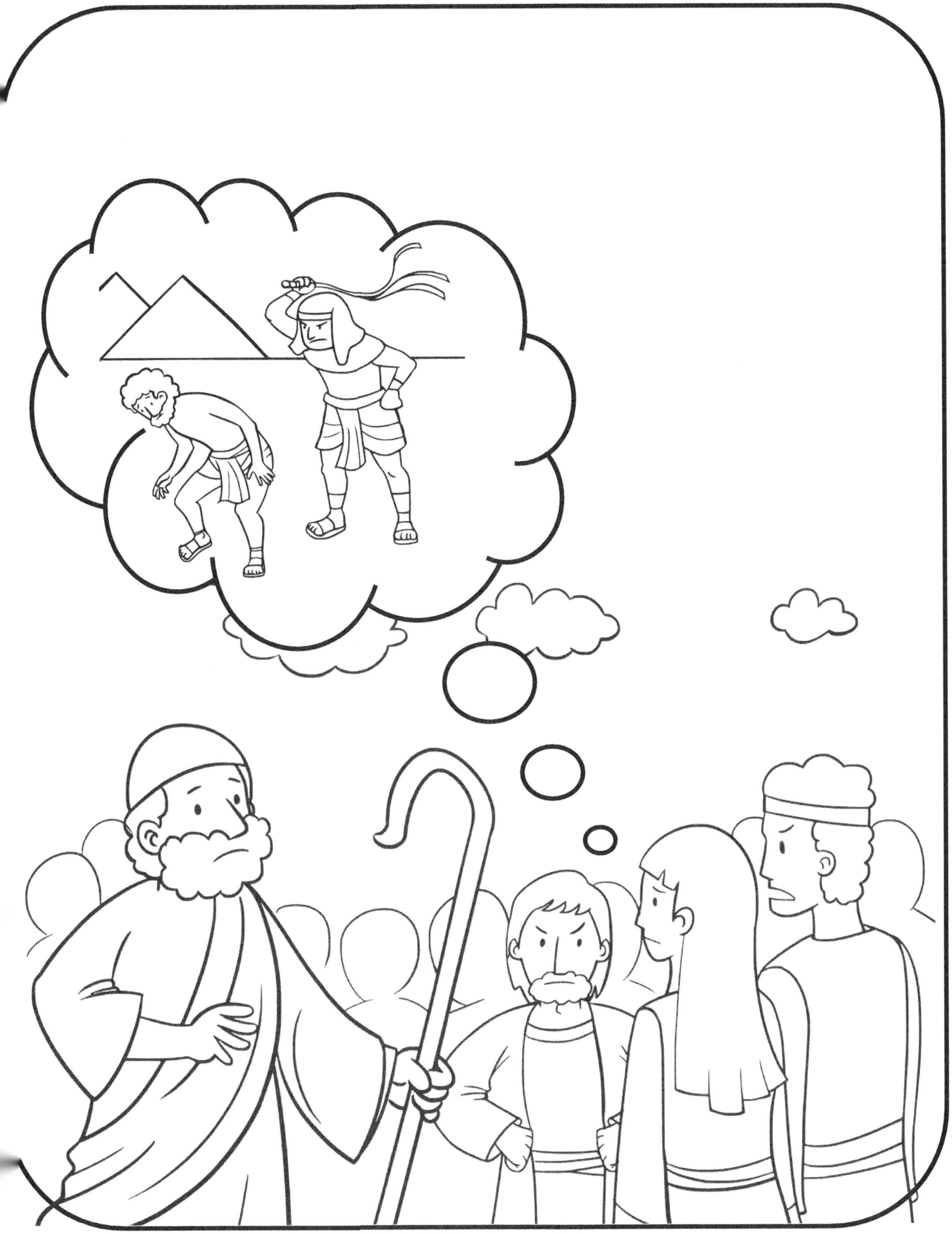

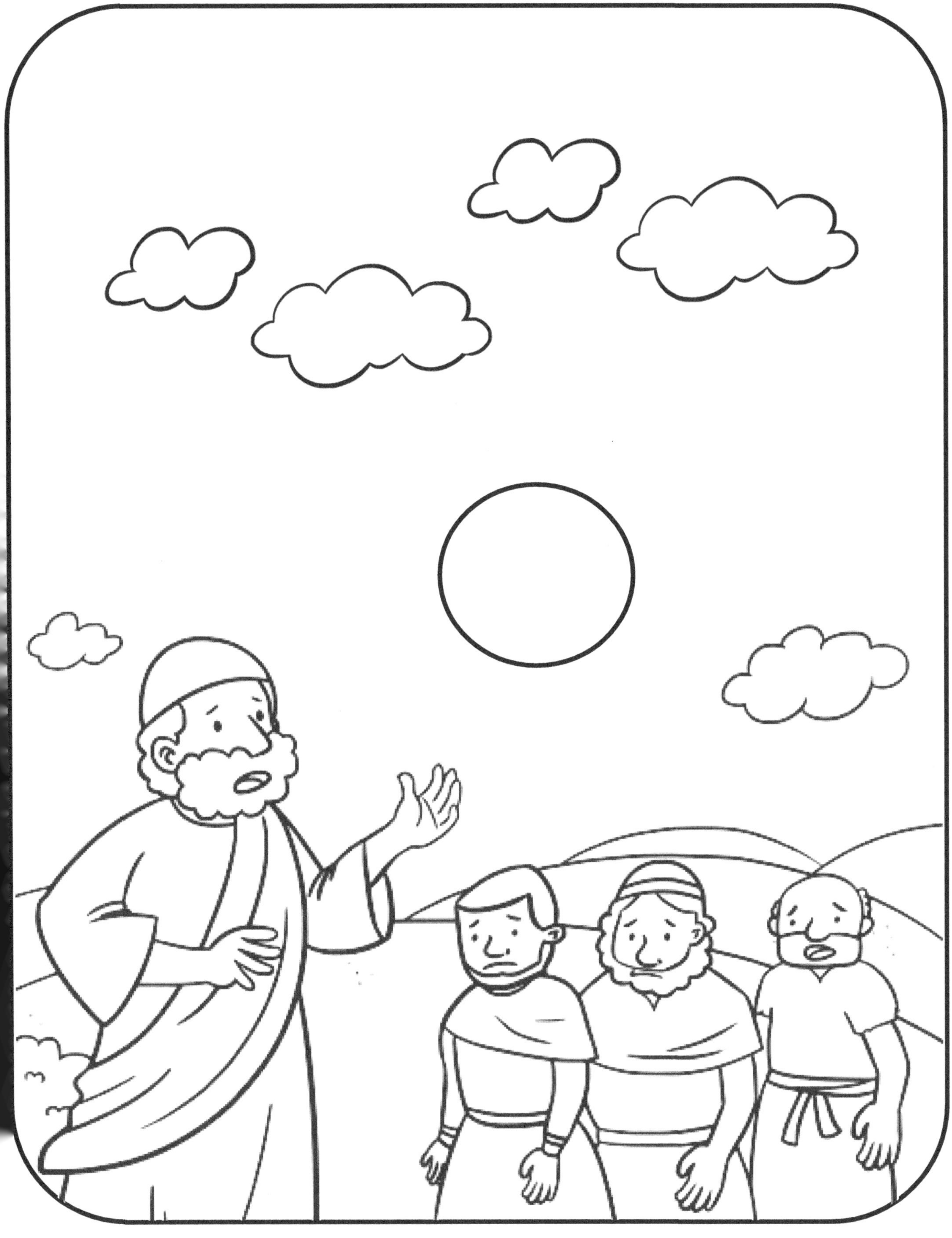

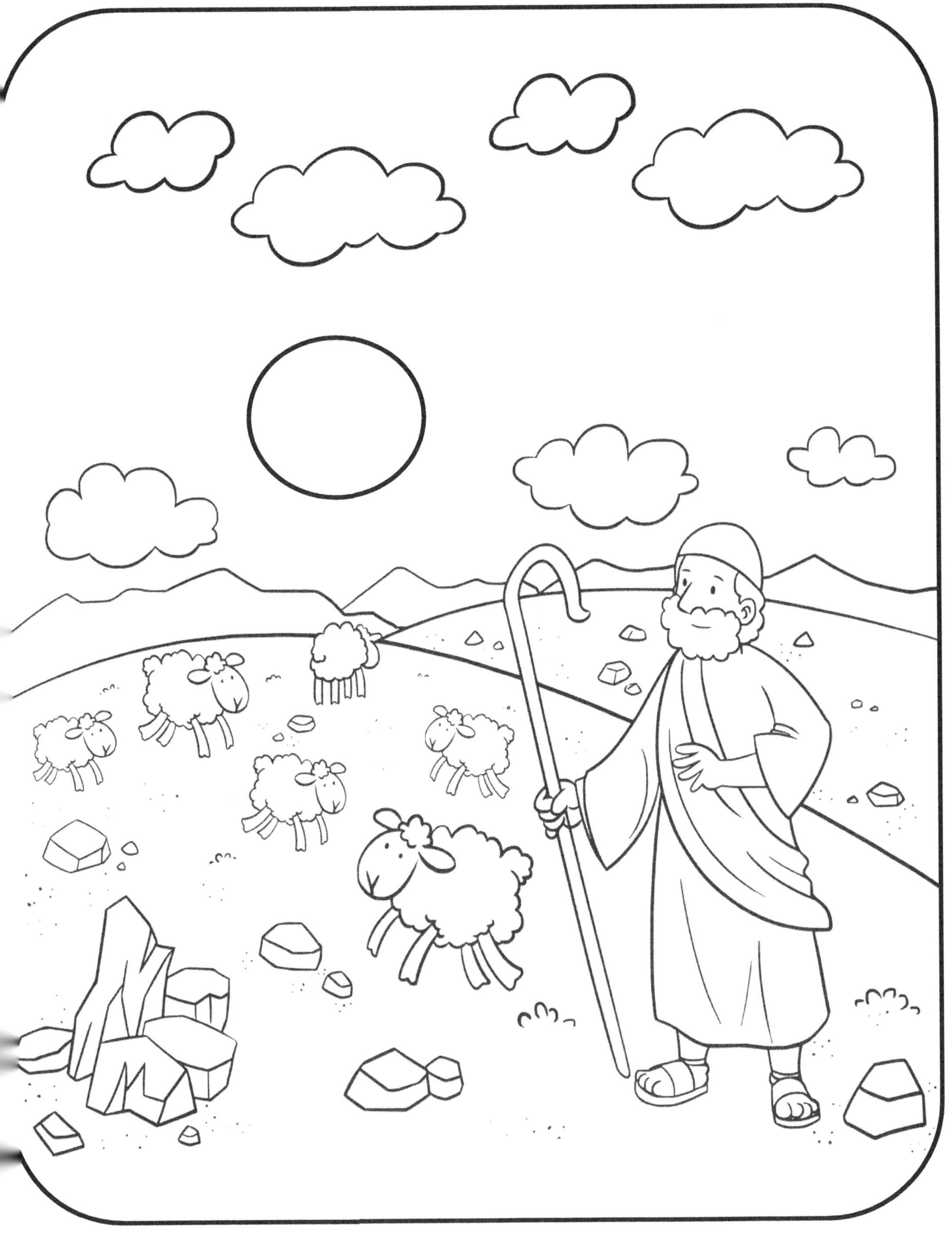

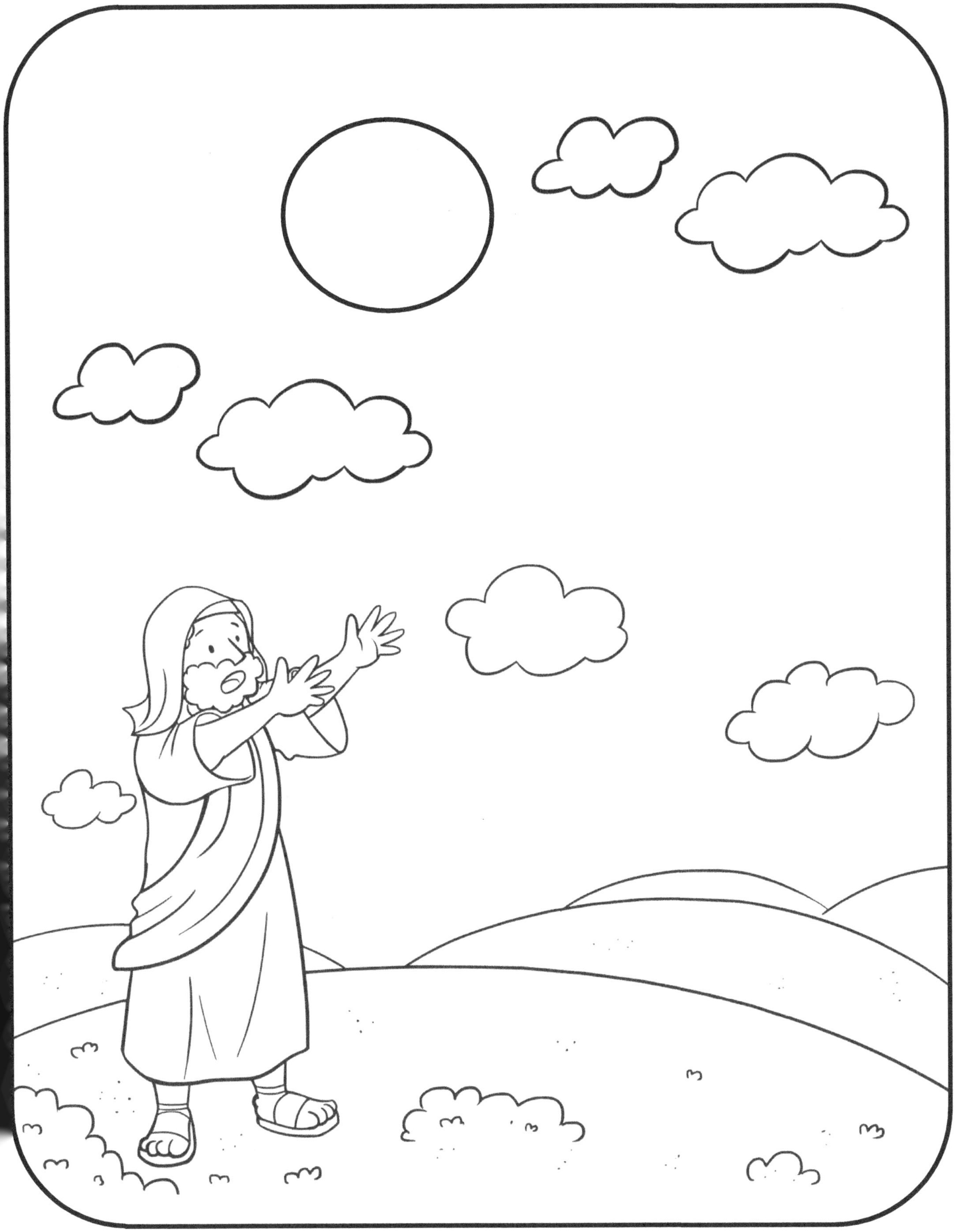

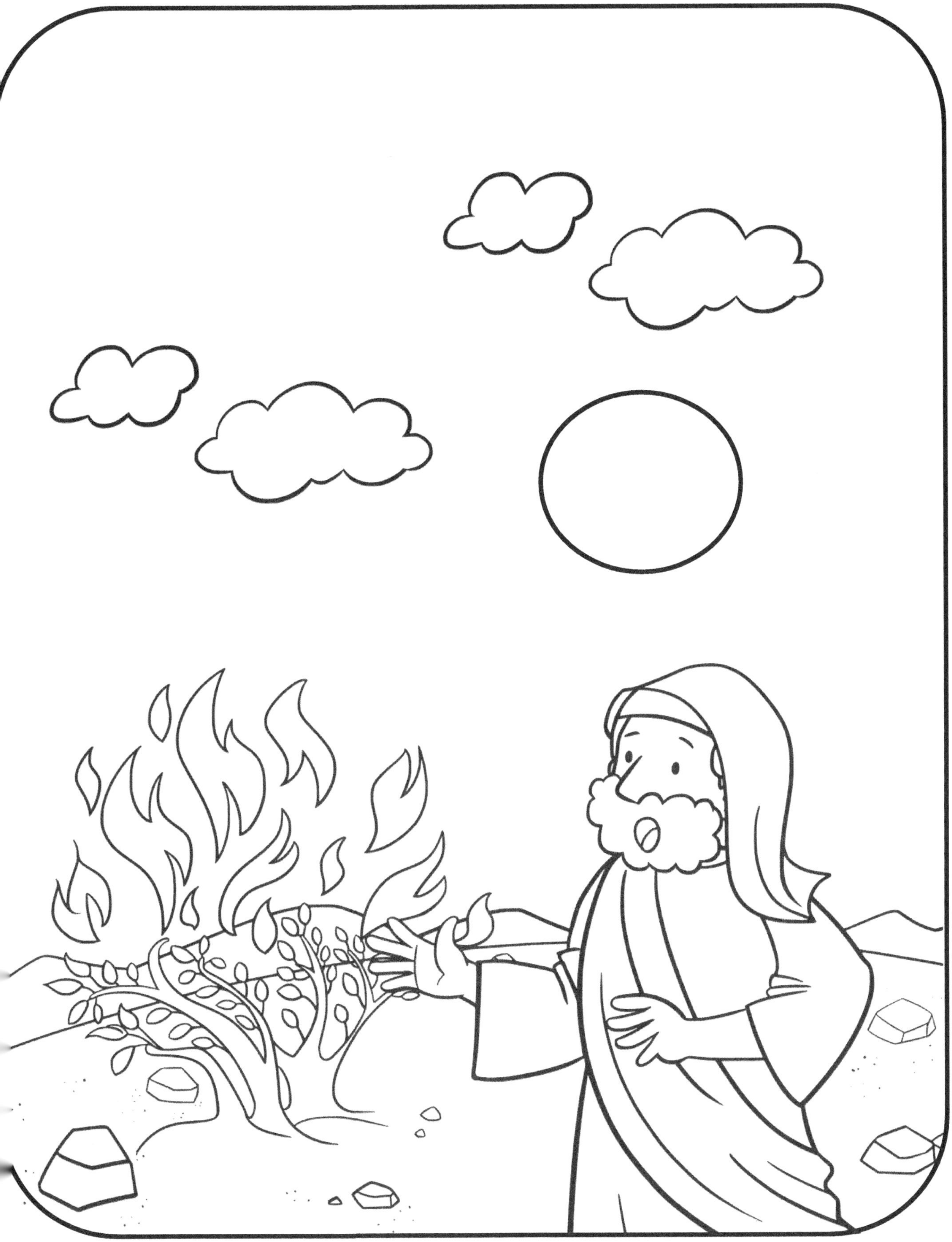

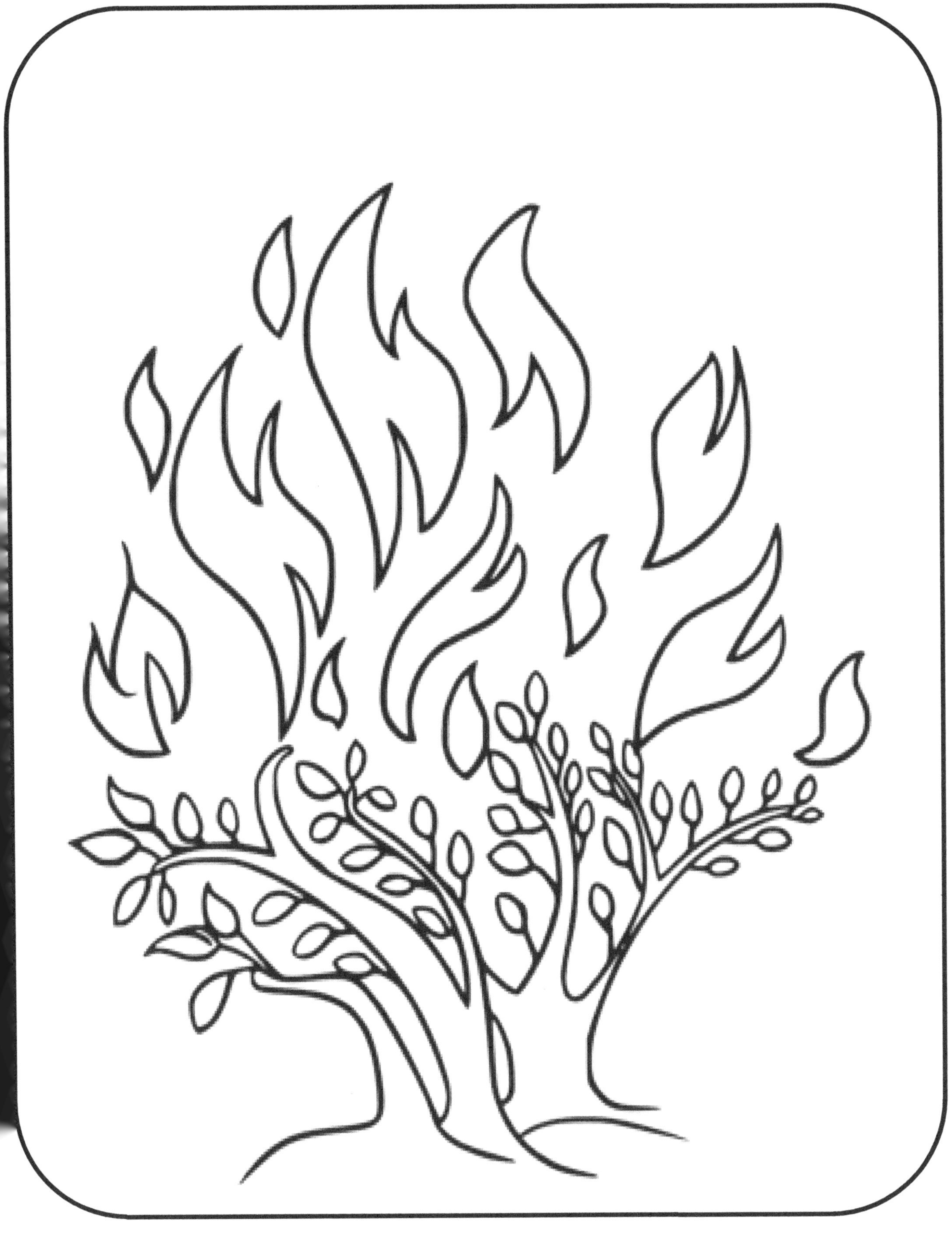

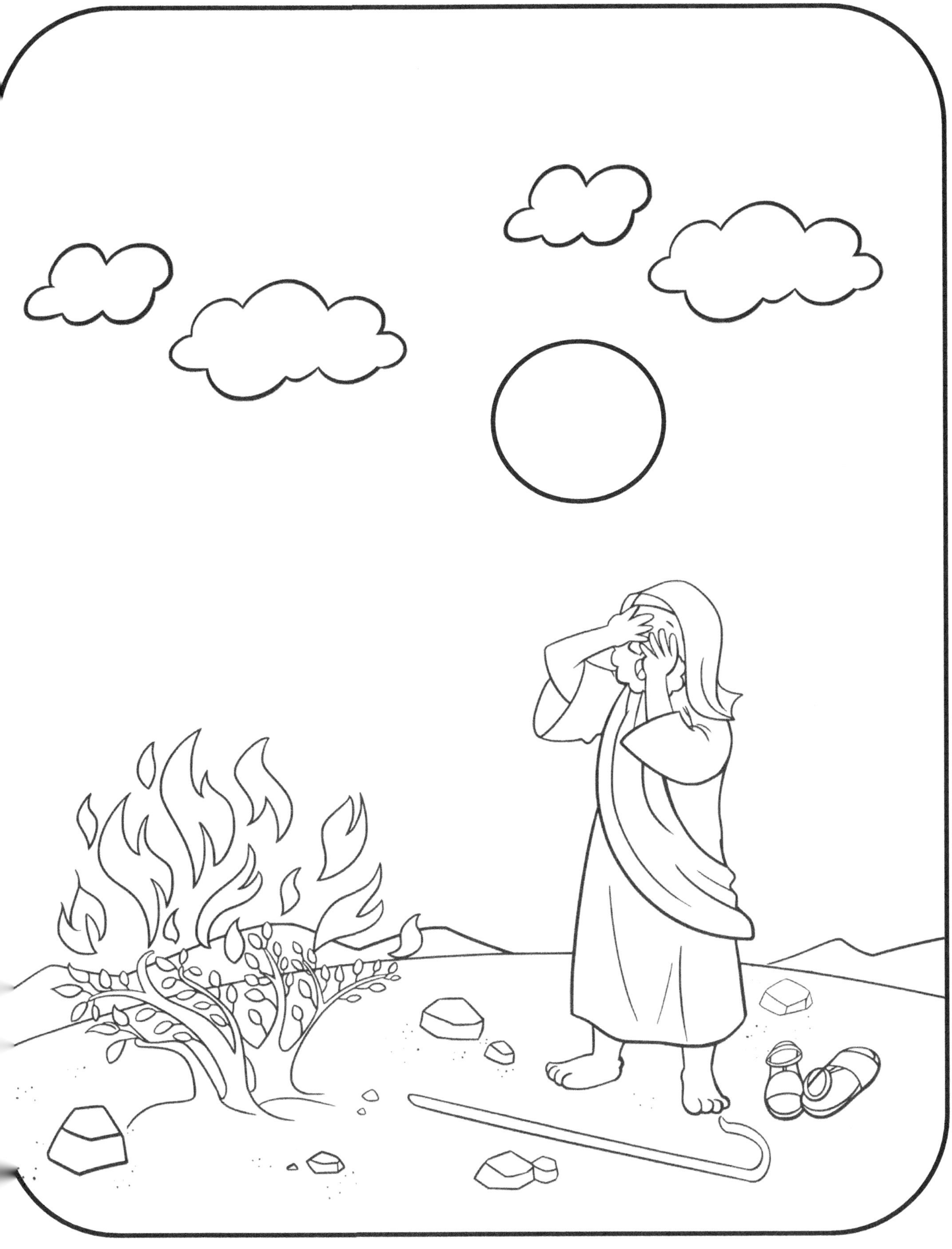

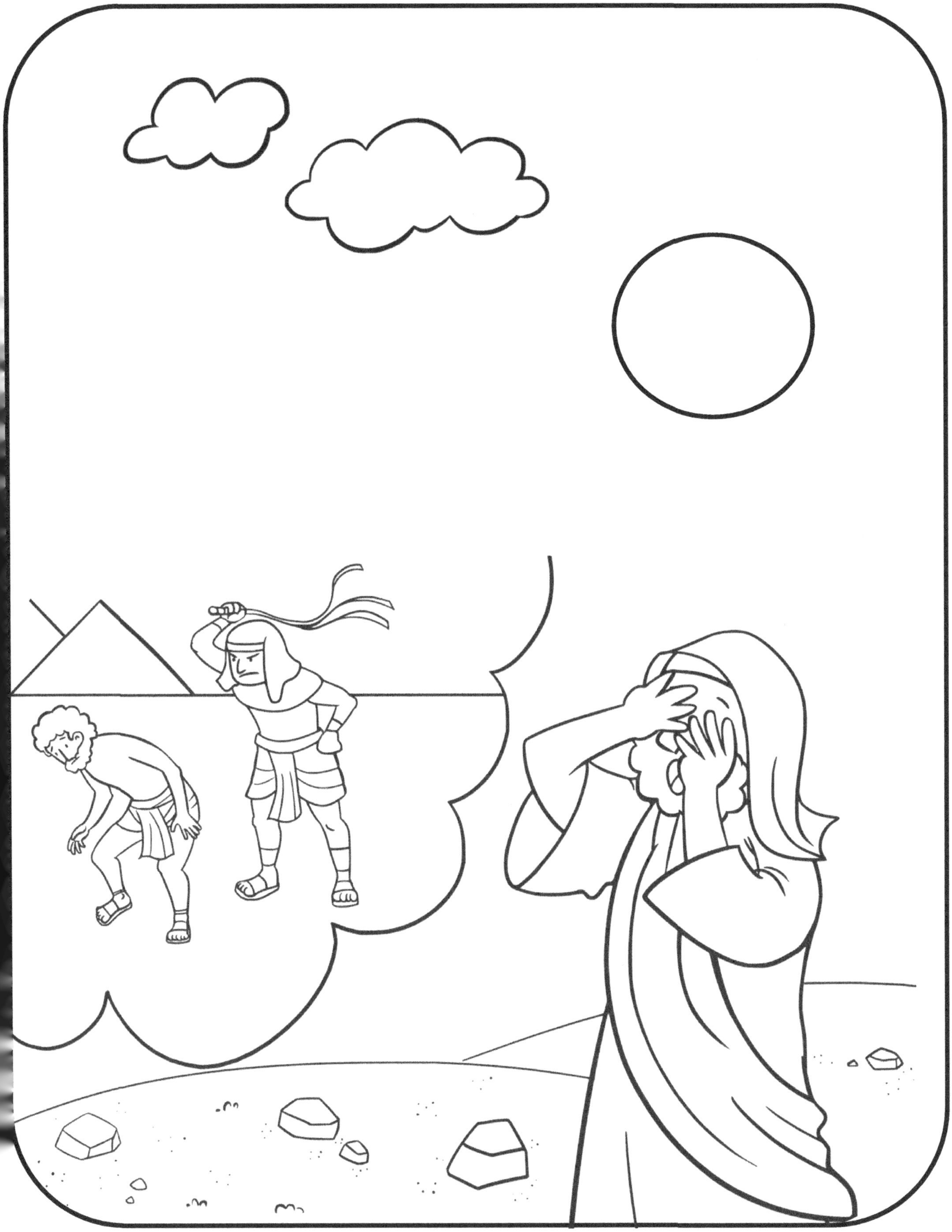

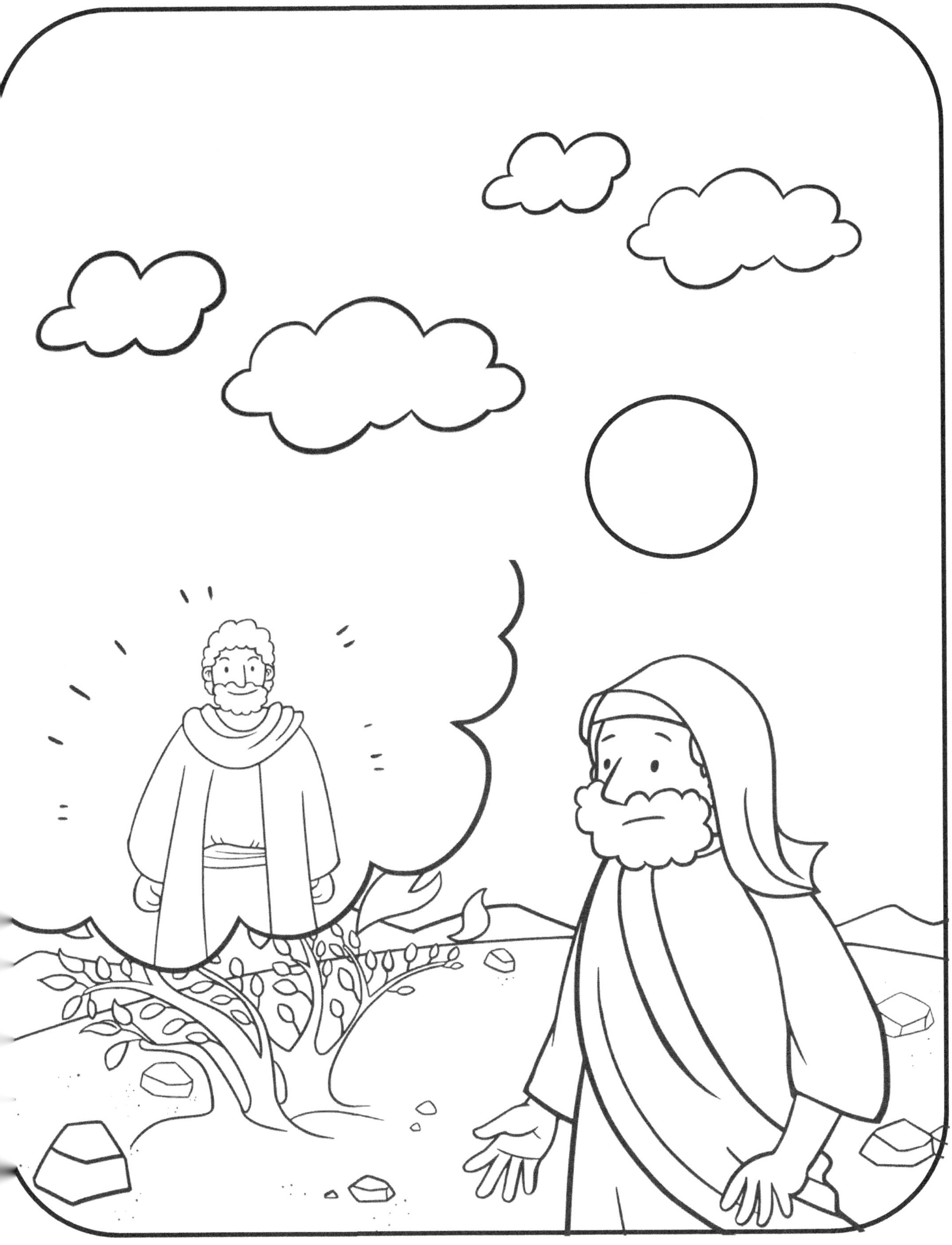

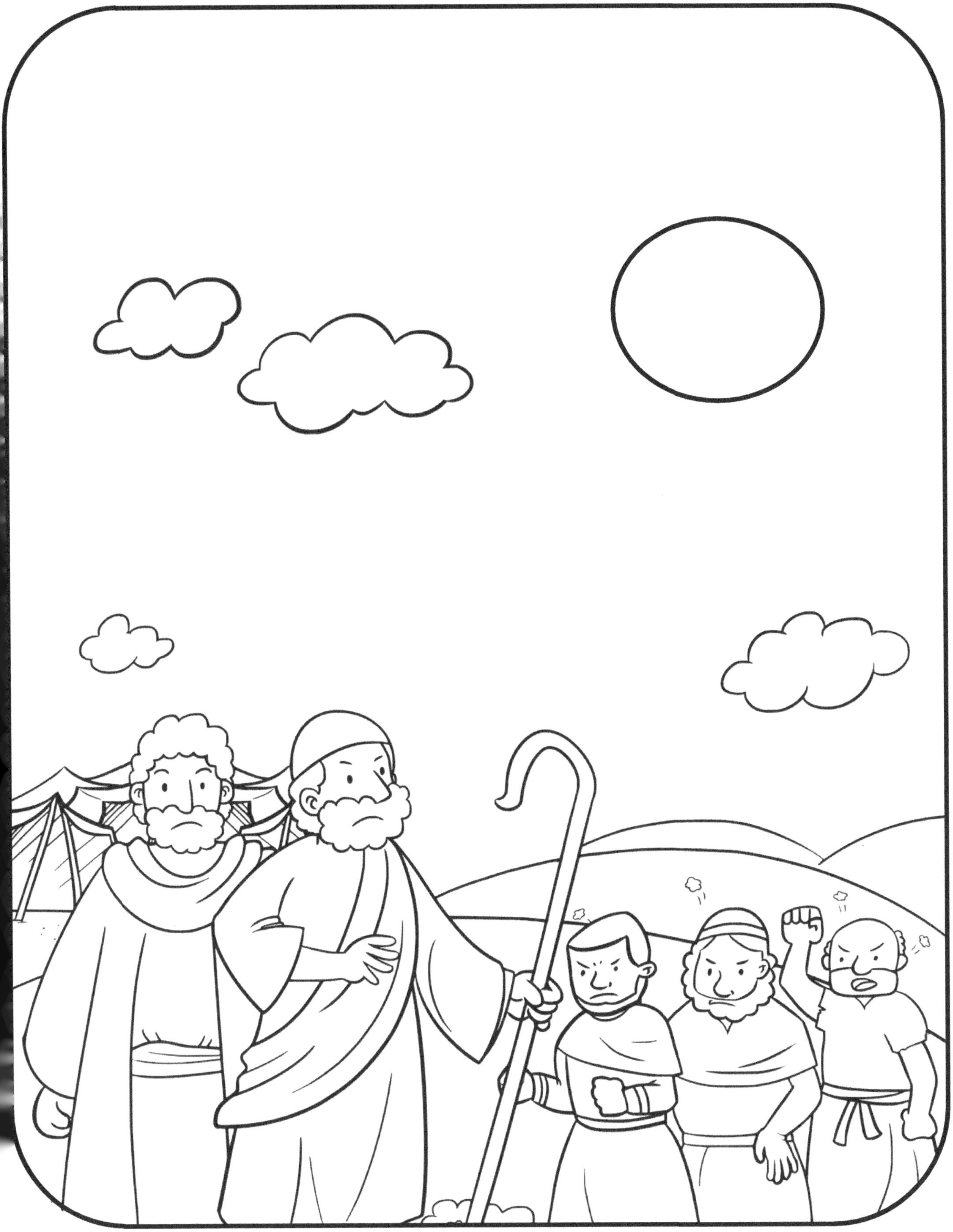

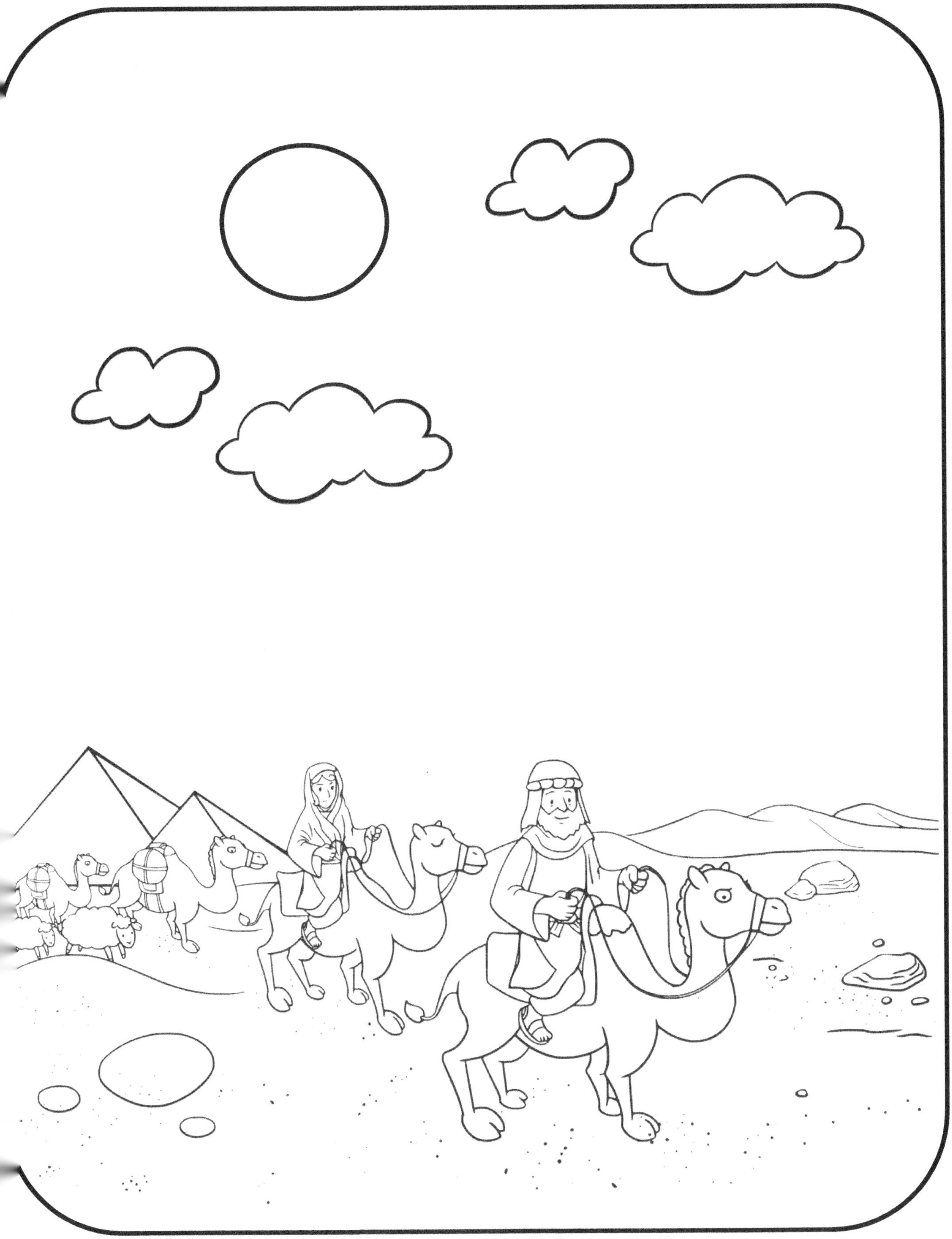

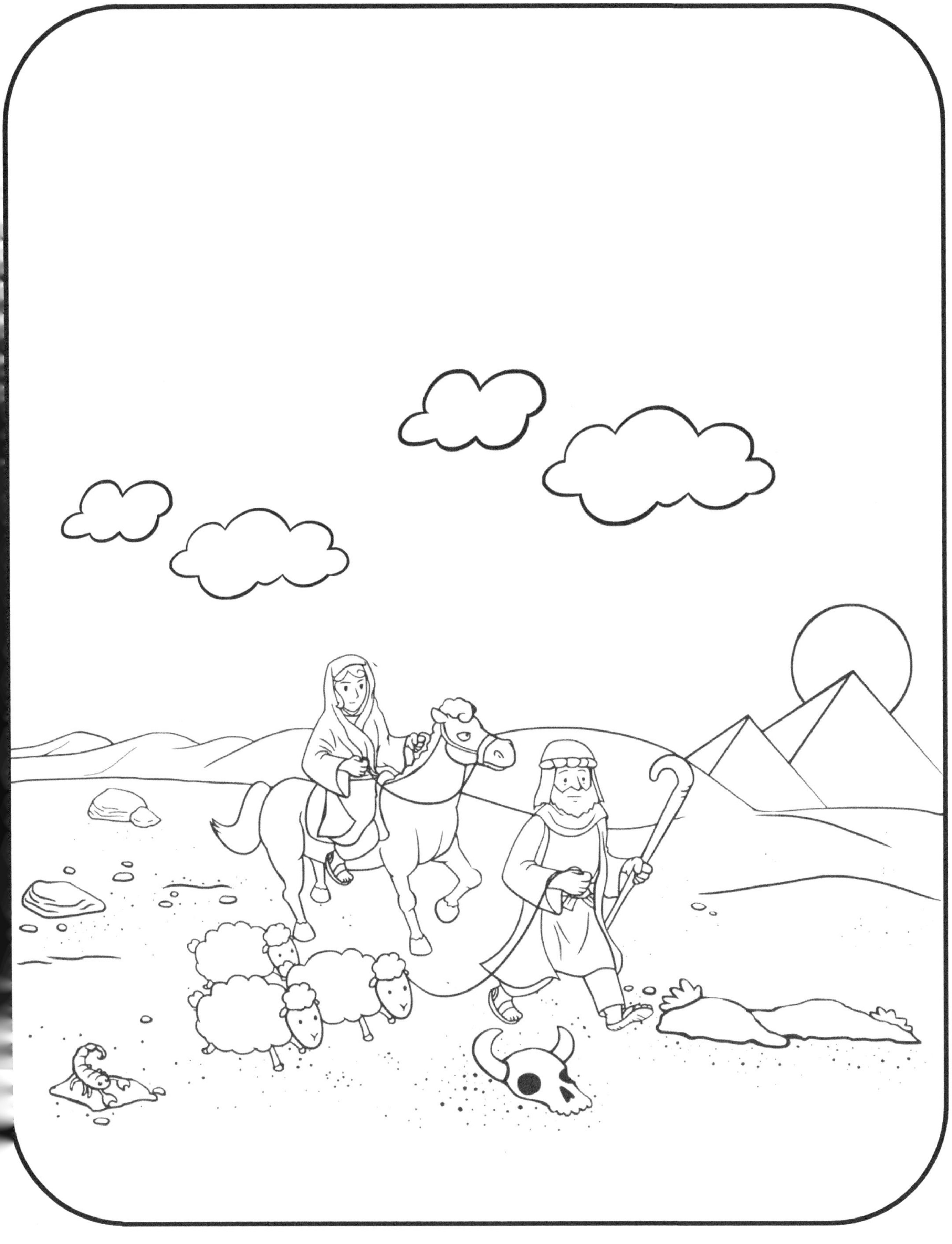

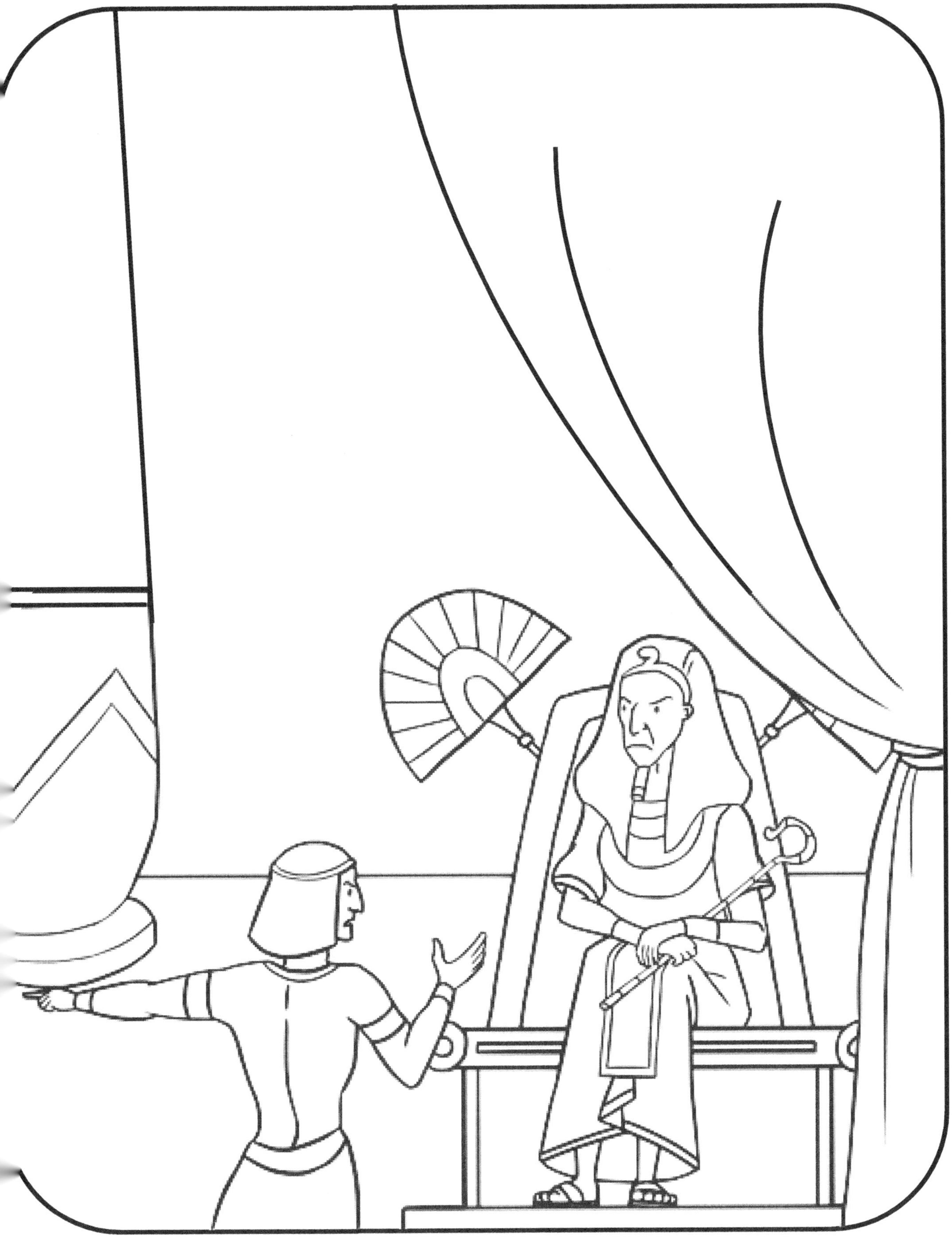

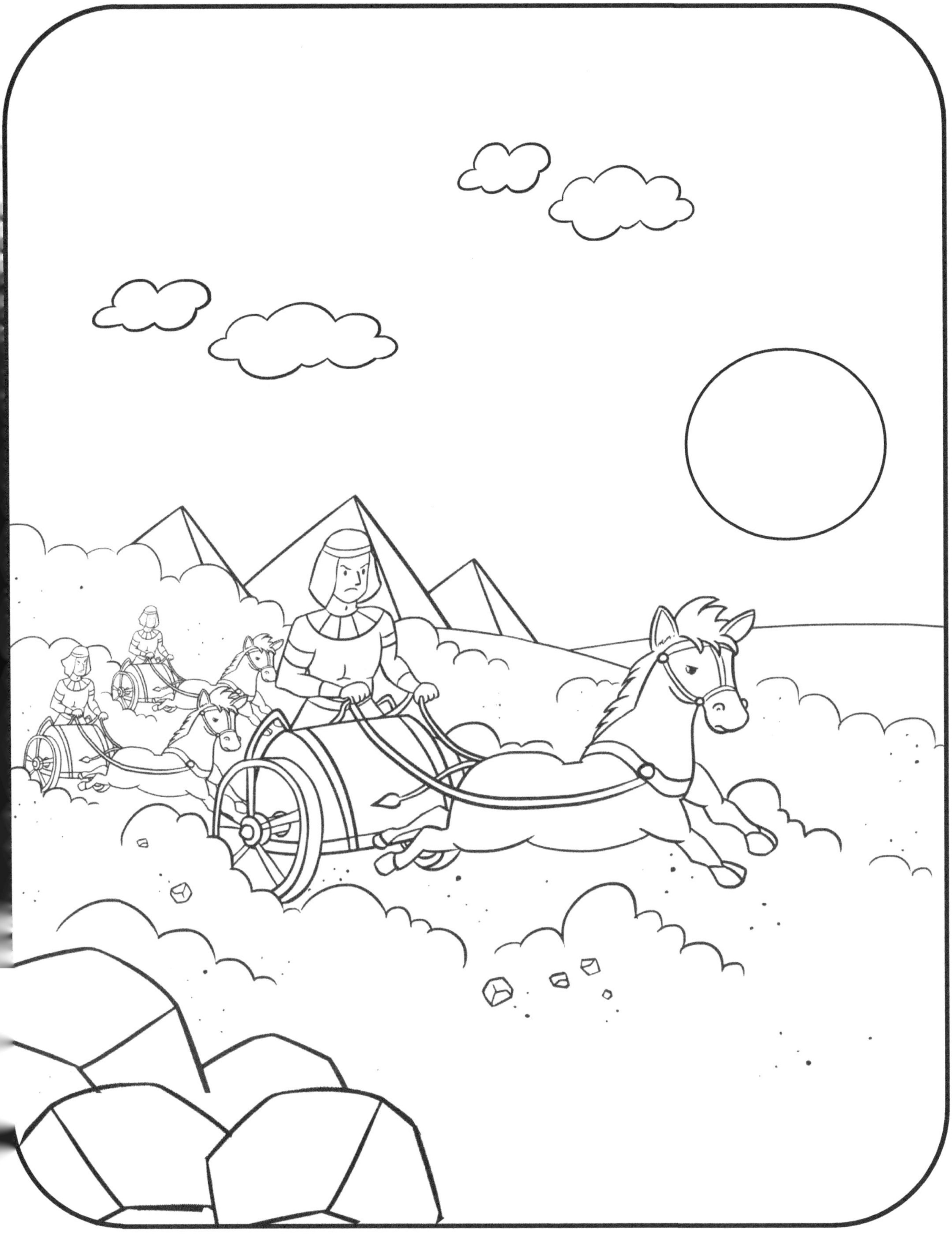

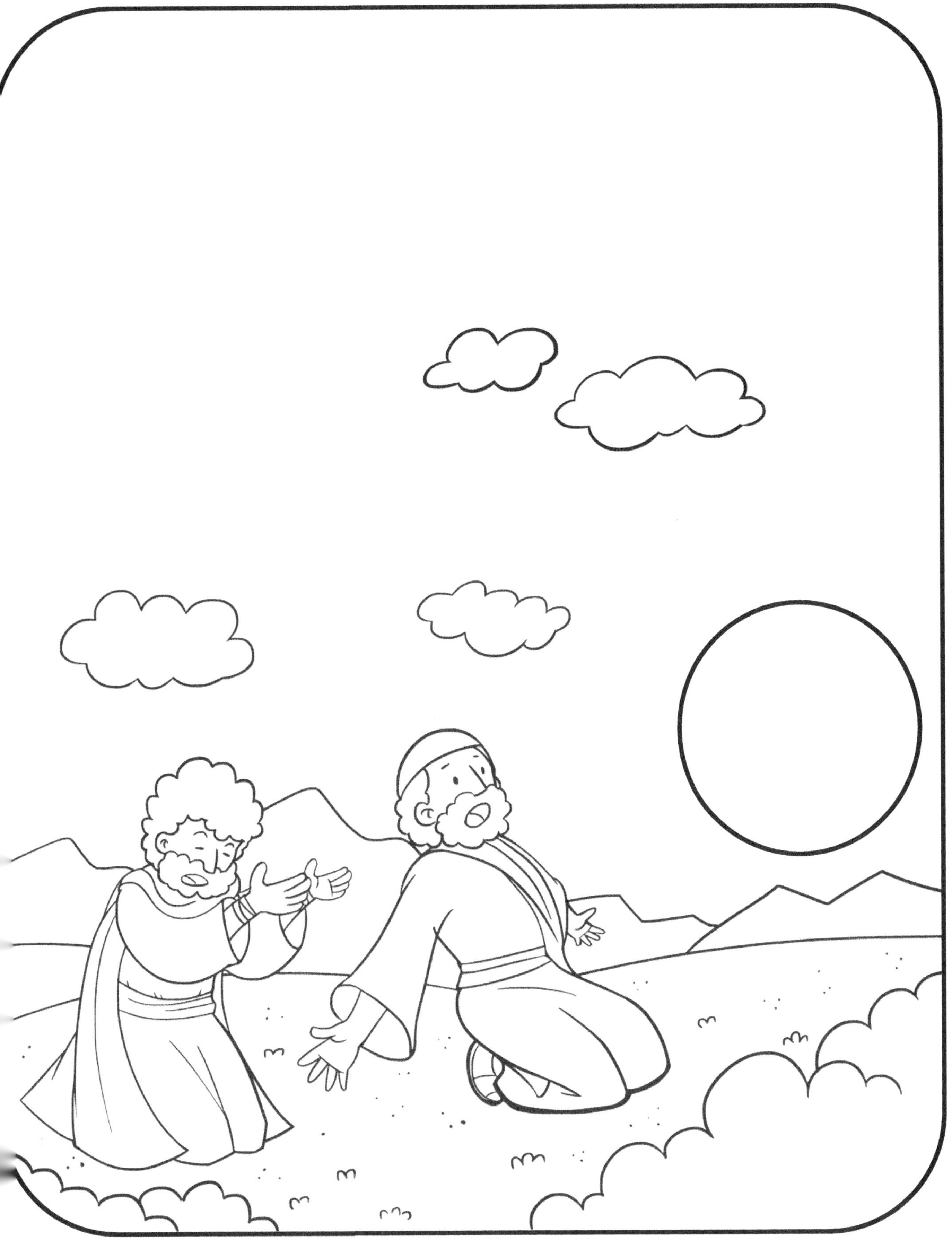

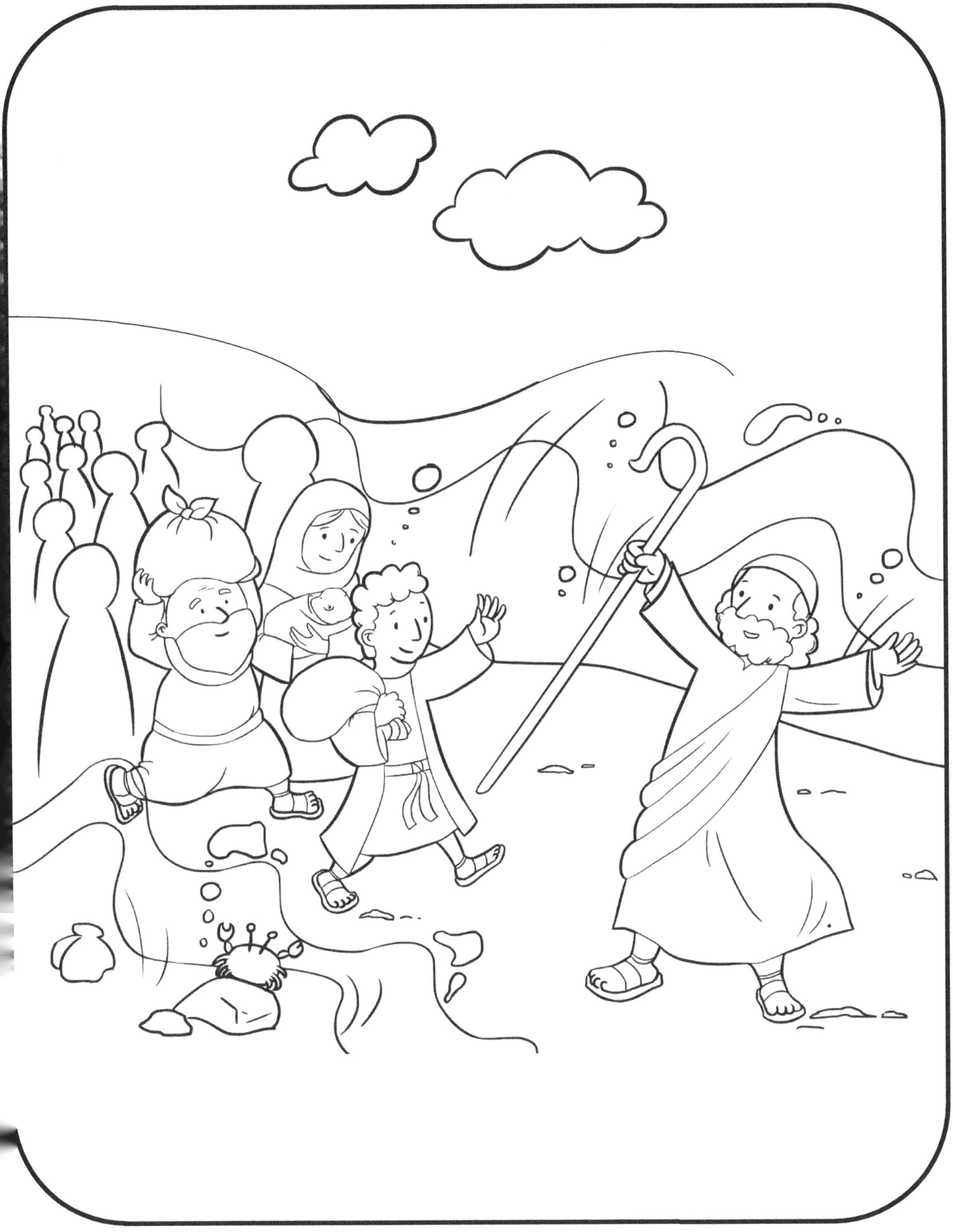

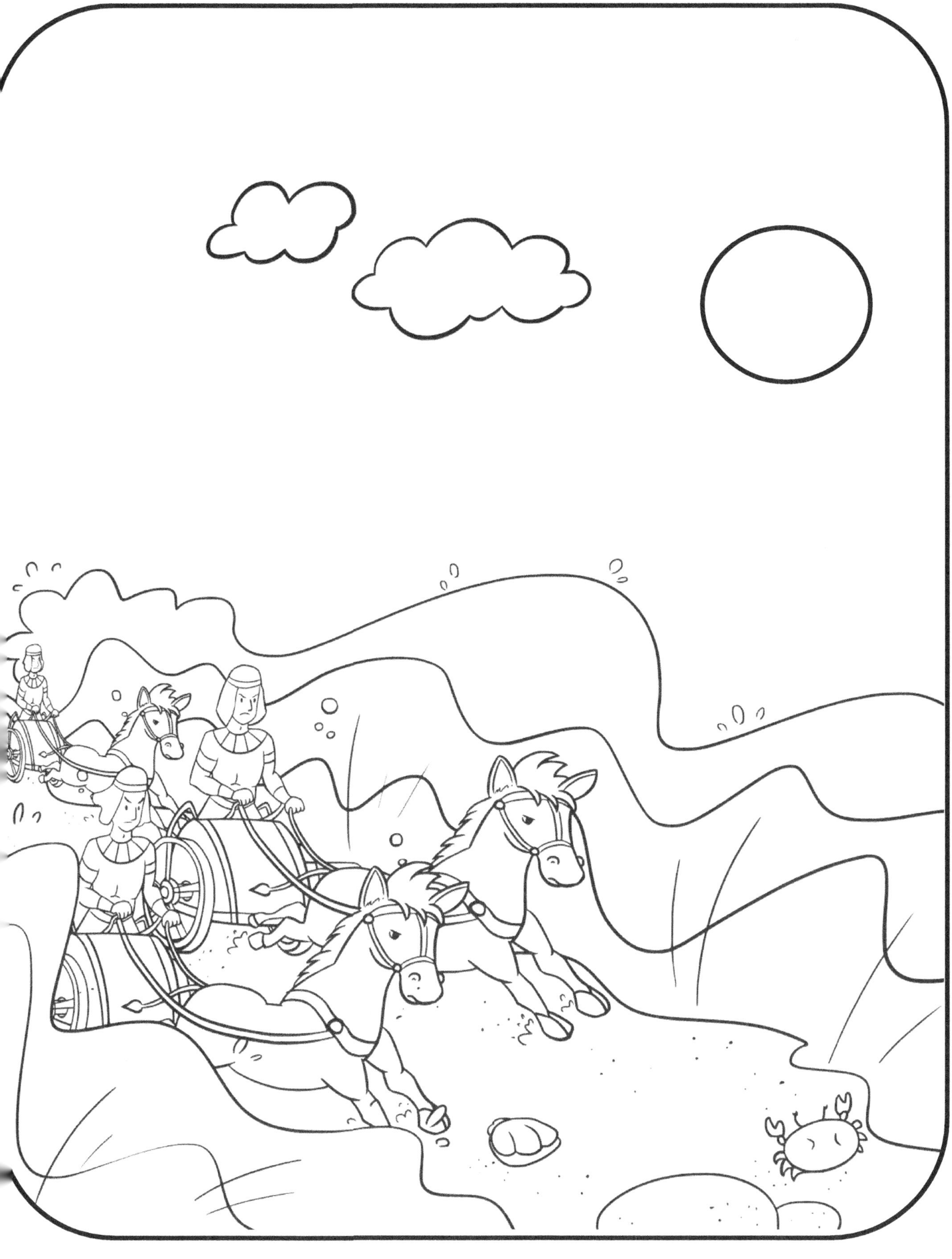

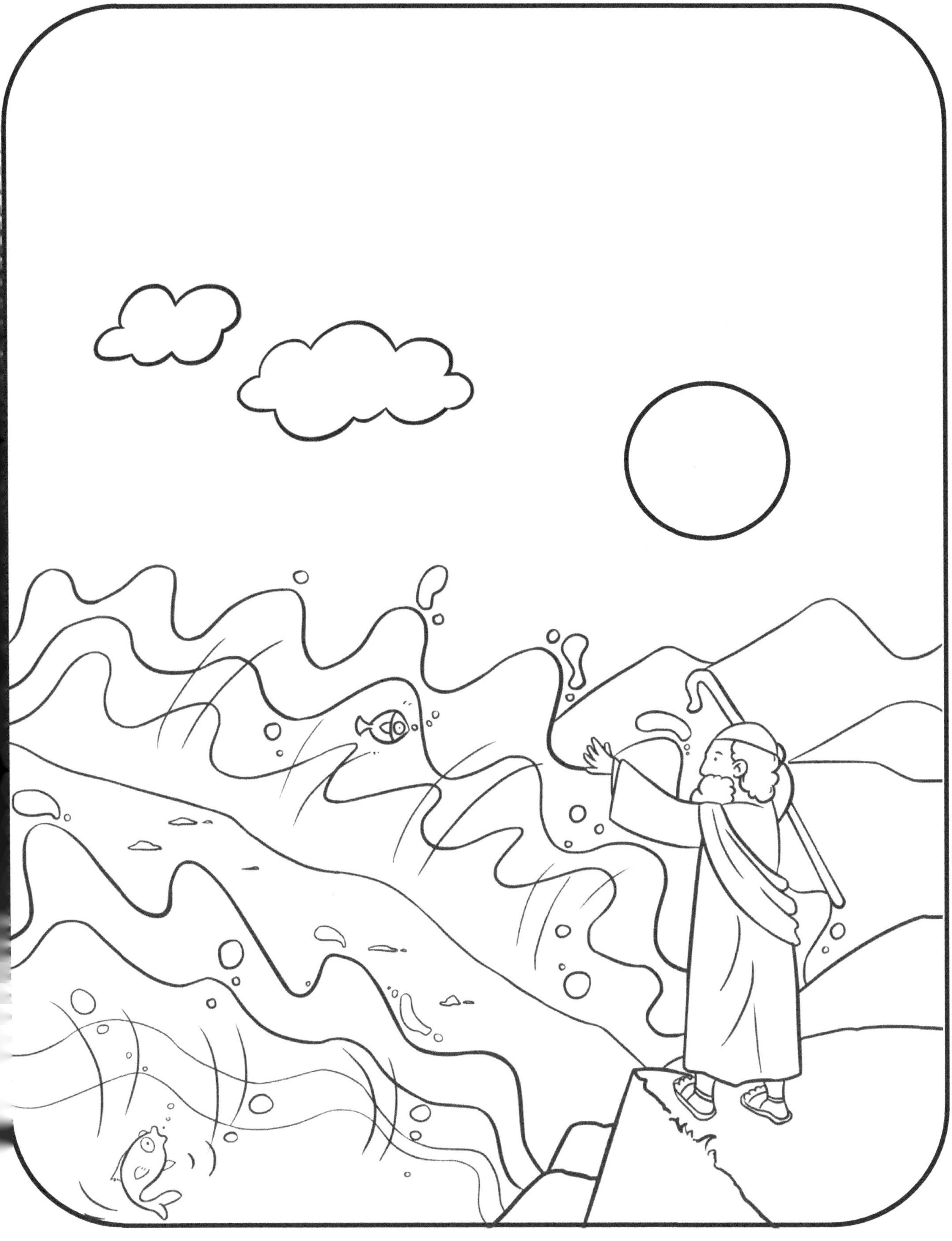

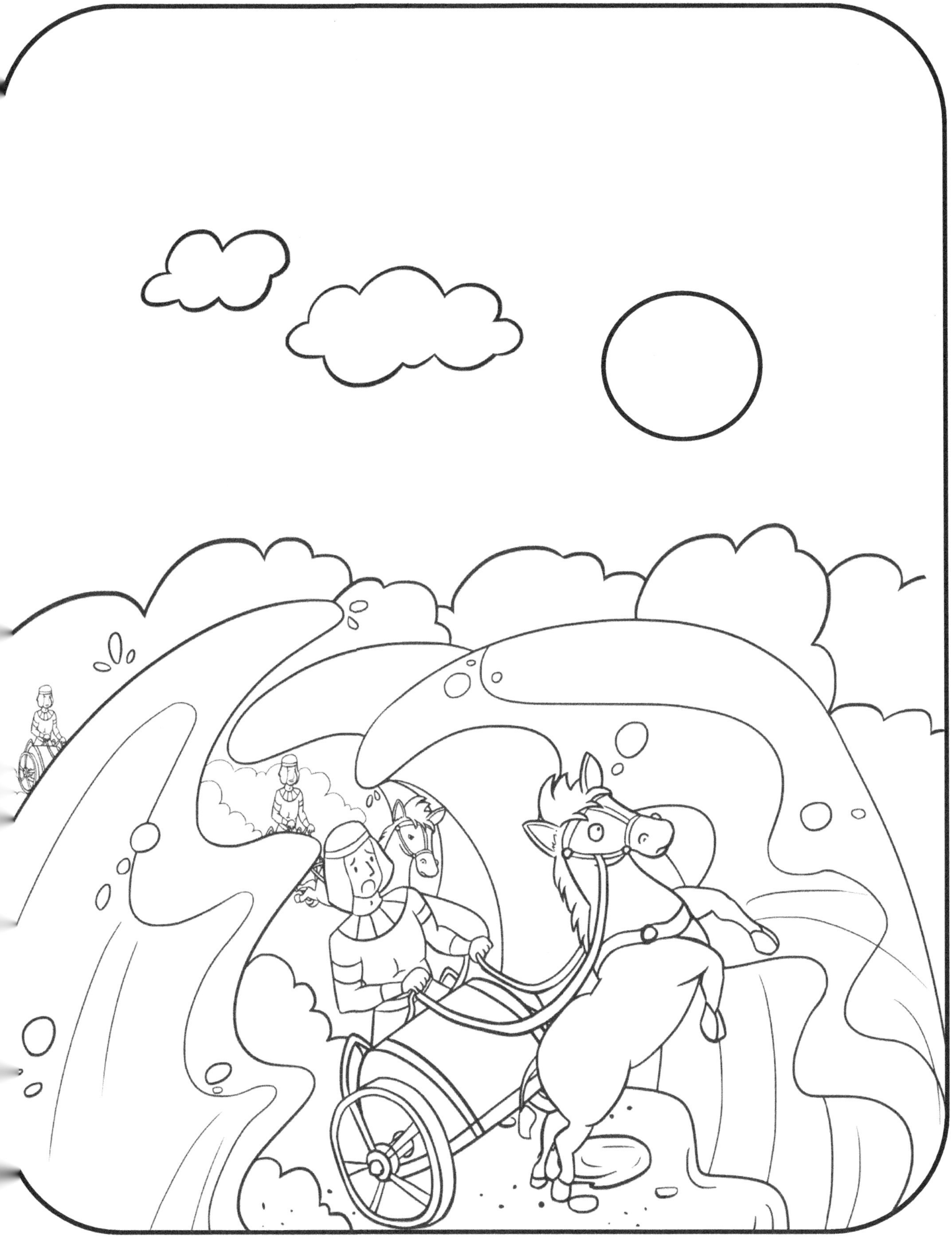

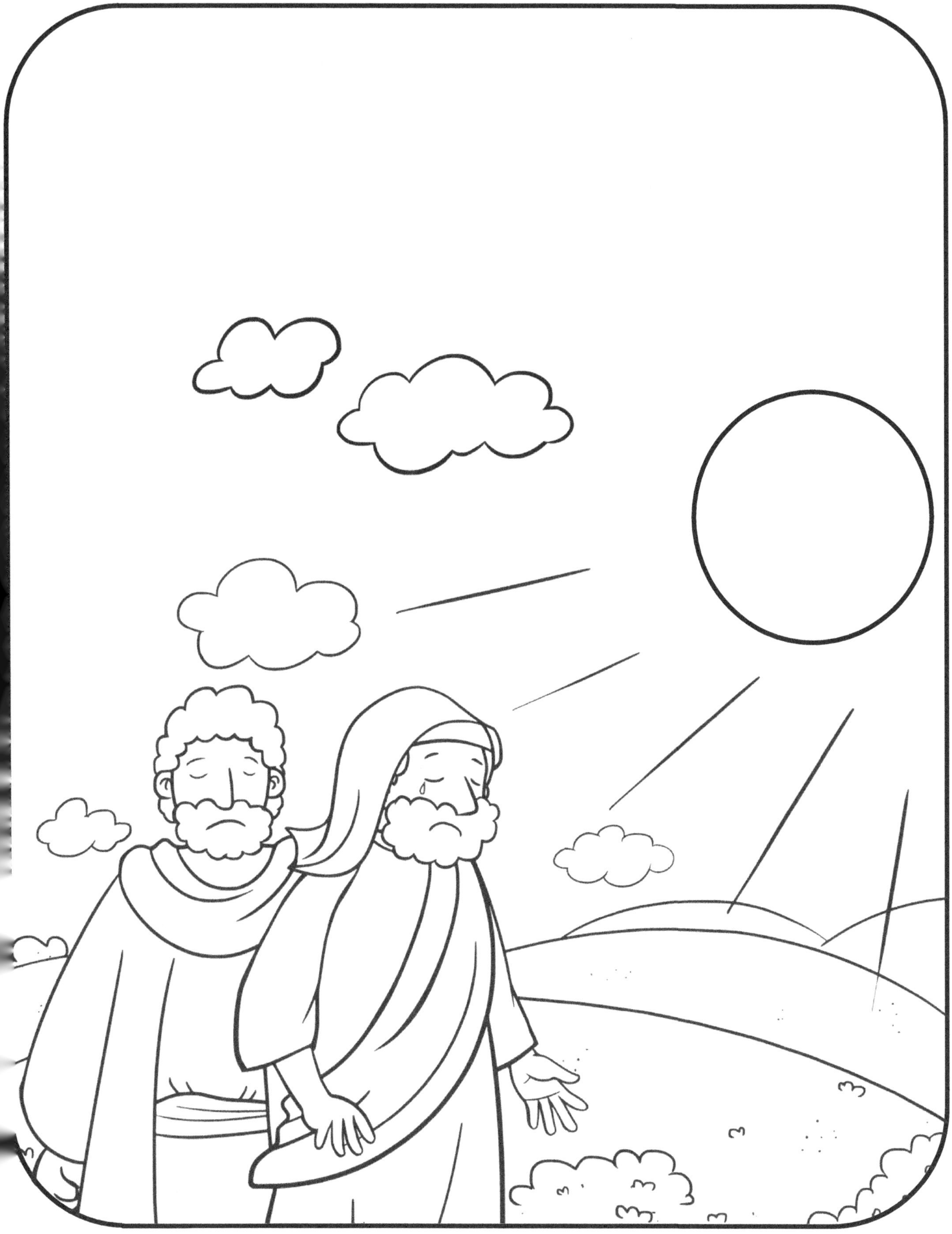

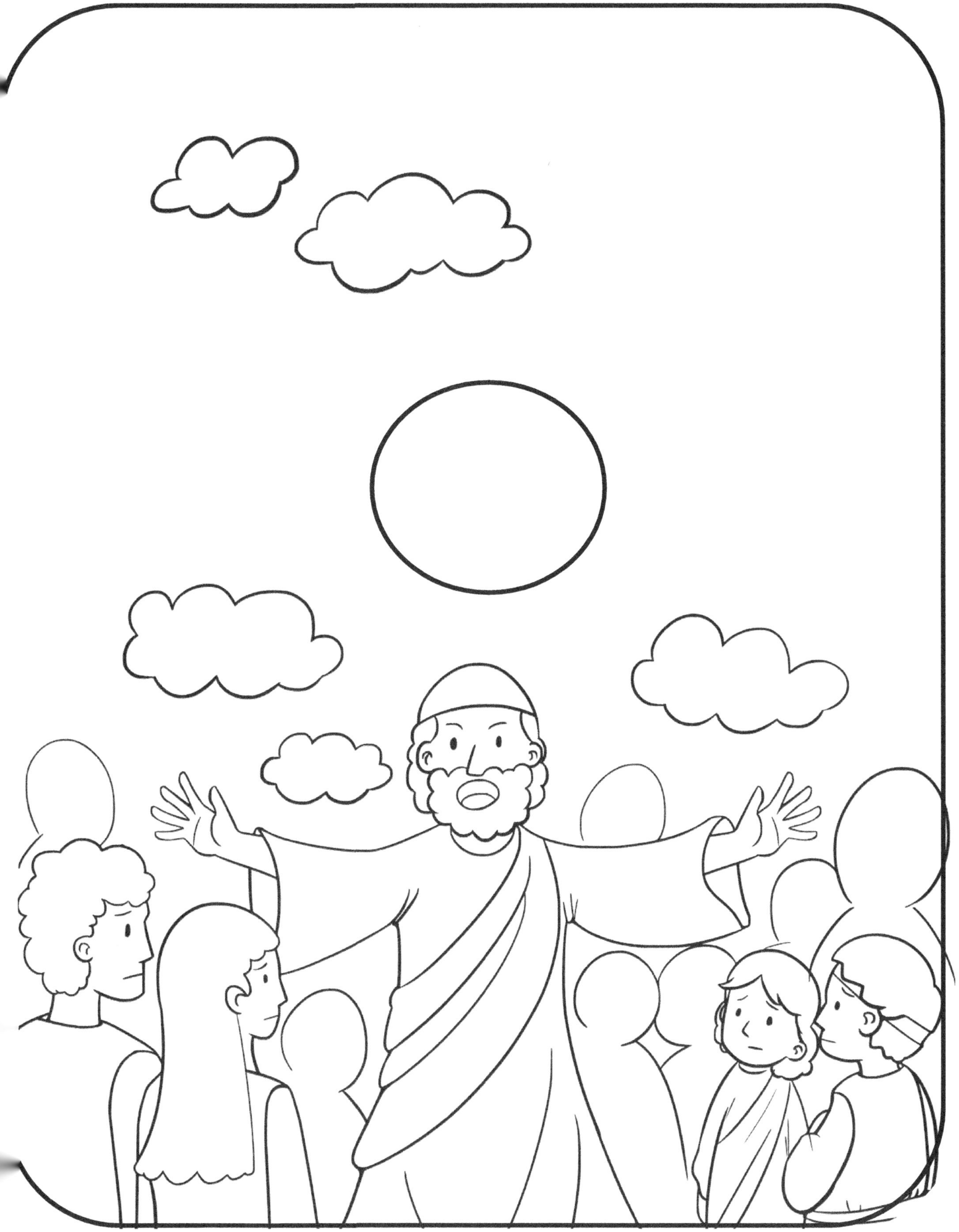

Made in the USA
Las Vegas, NV
03 March 2025

19008697R00031